James Watt

Neil Champion

H **www.heinemann.co.uk**
Visit our website to find out more information about **Heinemann Library** books.

To order:
☎ Phone 44 (0) 1865 888066
📄 Send a fax to 44 (0) 1865 314091
💻 Visit the Heinemann Bookshop at www.heinemann.co.uk to browse our catalogue and order online.

First published in Great Britain by Heinemann Library,
Halley Court, Jordan Hill, Oxford OX2 8EJ
a division of Reed Educational and Professional Publishing Ltd.
Heinemann is a registered trademark of Reed Educational & Professional Publishing Ltd.

OXFORD MELBOURNE AUCKLAND
JOHANNESBURG BLANTYRE GABORONE
IBADAN PORTSMOUTH (NH) USA CHICAGO

20883
509.2

Designed by AMR
Originated by Ambassador Litho Ltd
Printed in Hong Kong/China

ISBN 0 431 10447 6
04 03 02 01 00
10 9 8 7 6 5 4 3 2 1

British Library Cataloguing in Publication Data
Champion, Neil
James Watt. – (Groundbreakers)
1. Watt, James, 1736–1819 – Juvenile literature
2. Engineers – Scotland – Biography – Juvenile literature
I. Title
621.1'092

Acknowledgements
The publishers would like to thank the following for permission to reproduce photographs:
Ann Ronan Picture Library: pp. 15, 20; Hulton Getty: pp. 8, 12, 21, 31, 33, 37; J. Allan Cash Ltd: p. 42; Katz Pictures Ltd: pp. 6, 26; Mary Evans Picture Library: pp. 9, 11, 30, 35, 41; Science Museum/Science & Society Picture Library: pp. 7, 13, 18, 19, 21, 23, 24, 25, 27, 28, 32, 36, 38, 39; The Bridgeman Art Library: pp. 4, 5, 10, 14, 16, 17, 22, 29, 34, 43.

Cover photograph reproduced with permission of the Science Photo Library.

Every effort has been made to contact copyright holders of any material reproduced in this book. Any omissions will be rectified in subsequent printings if notice is given to the publishers.

Any words appearing in the text in bold, **like this**, are explained in the glossary.

Contents

James Watt – a pioneer of steam   4

James Watt's early years   6

School days   8

London life and instrument-making   10

Glasgow University   12

Marriage, and the steam engine   14

Early forms of power   16

A short history of steam   18

Watt's separate condenser   20

Family and money matters   22

Disappointment and tragedy   24

A productive partnership   26

Interconnections   28

Steam power takes off   30

Rotary motion and other improvements   32

Measuring energy   34

Impact on industry and society   36

A rival engineer – Richard Trevithick   38

Old age and contentment   40

The legacy of James Watt   42

Timeline   44

Places to visit and further reading   45

Glossary   46

Index   48

James Watt – a pioneer of steam

This painting, The Wagon *by Thomas Gainsborough (1727–88), shows the landscape Watt grew up in. It was largely rural, with small towns and villages linked by rough roads.*

James Watt was born in Scotland in 1736. His future career was to make him one of the country's leading engineers and inventors. He was to play a vital part in bringing the **Industrial Revolution** to its full potential, by designing machines that used the power of steam more effectively than ever before. However, at the time that he was born, life went on essentially as it had done for hundreds of years. Most people lived in villages and small towns and worked on the land, in small-scale crafts, and in trade. Inventions in science and engineering had brought about some changes, but these were generally isolated and had little impact on people's lives. Farming, mining, cloth-making, printing and transport all operated in a way that a medieval time-traveller would have recognized. In fact, some aspects of life had not changed for thousands of years. A Roman legionary in the 5th century, for example, could have made the journey from Watt's home town of Greenock to London in the same time that it took Watt himself to make that journey in 1755 – twelve gruelling days on horseback!

Sources of energy

One of the main reasons for the lack of change was the fact that sources of energy were the same for an Ancient Roman, a medieval peasant, and an 18th-century farmer. These sources were wind, water, and the muscles of people and of animals such as horses. But wind and water are unreliable and muscle power is limited. Technology based on them could not change very greatly. Watermills, windmills and horse-powered machinery had led to some improvements in agriculture and the production of tools and cloth, but those improvements were restricted by the nature of the power source.

The importance of steam power

When people started to learn how to use the power of steam, in the late 17th century, development shifted up a few gears. Steam power was to provide an energy source unlike the others – it was relatively reliable and portable, it always kept going, and it went way beyond muscle, wind and water power in terms of its sheer output. It would quickly provide hundreds of times more power than a horse ever could and it did not become tired.

James Watt's role

The key to making full use of steam lay in controlling its incredible power. This meant making it safe to use. It meant designing machines capable of various tasks to meet various needs (of mine-owners, textile manufacturers, printers, and eventually train and boat operators), and providing efficient use of that energy.

James Watt lived at a vital time in the development of steam power. Engineers before him had realized its potential and built machines that used its power. However, Watt was to be crucial in designing machines that were far better suited to the jobs they had to do. In the early stages, this meant pumping water from coal and tin mines in Britain. In partnership with the businessman Matthew Boulton, Watt made steam-powered machinery available to many mine-owners, farmers and textile producers. This combination of practical science and industry was the very ingredient that fuelled the Industrial Revolution.

This painting, Winter Landscape by George Smith (1741–76), shows a water wheel, which was a common sight in rural Britain in the 18th century.

James Watt's early years

An engraving of Port Glasgow, on the River Clyde. Watt was brought up in a port on the same river, at Greenock.

James Watt was born in the small Scottish port of Greenock, on the River Clyde, west of Glasgow. His father had trained as a carpenter and **shipwright**, but had expanded his business and made a comfortable income. He bought shares in ships and traded in ventures abroad, though he also was skilled in making fine instruments for navigation, such as telescopes, compasses and **quadrants**.

When James was born on 19 January 1736, he was treated with great care. His mother had lost several babies already and was determined not to let this one fall prey to the high **infant mortality** that existed at the time. He was not a strong boy, and needed the extra care and attention. He suffered acute **migraines**, vicious headaches that would plague him at least for the early part of his life.

Home learning

Because of James's delicate health, his parents decided to begin his education at home. He did not go to school until he was 11. Both his parents were highly intelligent and they shared the role of educator. His grandfather had been a mathematics teacher, and in the house there was a picture of Isaac Newton, the English mathematician and scientist.

A painting of John Napier, the Scottish mathematician and inventor of **logarithms**, also graced the walls of the house. James's mother taught him to read. His father tackled mathematics and writing skills. Not surprisingly, he also bought James a carpentry set and showed him how to use the numerous instruments that it contained.

Signs of invention

James used his carpentry set to take his toys to pieces and rebuild them in different ways. Was this an early sign of his inclination towards inventing new objects and new ways of doing things? His home learning no doubt gave him great scope to develop as an individual, without having to compete with other children around him. All his life, he was to look at problems in a very personal way. His independence of thought and his strongly inquiring mind were nurtured by this unique form of education. This was one of the keys to his future success as an engineer and inventor.

But home learning had a downside – it left James a poor communicator. He did not get on with other people very easily. His natural shyness and timid nature were reinforced during his early years by his relative isolation. As we shall see, his future career could have been ruined by these traits in his personality. Luckily he was saved by the businessman Matthew Boulton, who was outward-looking, very positive and good at dealing with other people – all the things Watt was not.

The great Scottish mathematician John Napier. A painting such as this hung in Watt's family home, alongside one of Isaac Newton.

School days

The sheltered early life of James Watt came to an abrupt end in 1747 when he was sent off to school for the first time. He was 11 years old, but totally unprepared for the hurly-burly of his new environment. He became a natural target for the bullies, who no doubt saw him as something of an oddity. Physically, he could not stand up for himself; and mentally, he did not have the street-wise experience to turn attention away from himself or the canny instinct to get on the right side of the strongest boys. His only way out of this nightmare situation was to retreat further and further into himself. Going out into the wide world did not encourage him to come out of his shell; instead, the opposite happened.

How much his early experience at school laid the foundations for James's future pessimistic outlook on life is impossible to tell. But certainly it can have done little to help this already timid boy.

A class in progress in an 18th-century boys' school. Watt's class would have looked much like this.

This painting by Marcus Stone (1840–1921) portrays young James fascinated by the power of steam. Whether James was really so interested in steam as a boy is not certain.

Grammar school

At the age of 13, James moved to Greenock **Grammar School**. Here he found an atmosphere much more to his liking. Studies were encouraged and bullying ceased. This quiet, intellectual teenager could emerge a little and show what he was good at. He quickly developed in mathematics. He showed that he took after his father by displaying skill in making things from wood and metal. Within a few years, he had decided upon a career for himself – he wanted to be a scientific instrument-maker. He had seen many of the fine instruments for navigation that his father handled. Producing them would combine his mathematical ability with his skill in making practical and delicate objects.

There are several family tales about James Watt's boyhood that indicate his intellectual abilities. Some aim to show that he was fascinated by steam from an early age. This is what an aunt is quoted as saying to him:

'James, I never saw such an idle boy! … For the last half hour you have not spoken a word, but taken off the lid of that kettle and put it on again, holding now a cup and now a silver spoon over the steam; watching how it rises from the spout, and catching and counting the drops of water.'

There is even a painting by the artist Marcus Stone (above) that shows the young James sitting at a table with his parents, fascinated by steam rising from a kettle. How much truth there is in these tales is hard to know.

London life and instrument-making

James Watt left home at the age of 18. His plan was to go to Glasgow and train to become a scientific instrument-maker. He had already picked up considerable knowledge from his father. A distant relative on his mother's side was able to help him obtain temporary work at Glasgow University, under the scientist Professor Robert Dick. James helped lay out the specialist instruments for the professor to use. But the city itself proved a disappointment. There did not seem to be anyone ready or willing to take on a new **apprentice** to the trade. Watt worked for an optician for a while, but the position did not lead anywhere.

The move to London

Professor Dick recommended to Watt that he move to London to try to find the training he needed. Watt's father, whose business at this time was experiencing some setbacks, agreed to this. The professor contacted an instrument-maker in the capital, named James Short, and all seemed well. Watt arrived in June 1755, after a twelve-day journey on horseback, only to find that Short could not after all take him on. It also seemed that no one else could, either. He was no better off than he had been in Glasgow.

A painting by William Marlow (1740–1813) of mid-18th-century London, where Watt arrived after a twelve-day journey on horseback from Glasgow.

Cornhill, London, where James Watt worked 'to nine o'clock every night, except Saturdays,' training in the art of mathematical instrument-making.

Learning the trade

In London, the trade of instrument-making was governed by a **craft guild** called the **Worshipful Company of Clock-makers**. To qualify as an instrument-maker, and gain the benefits of guild membership, Watt would need to become apprenticed to a workshop. However, this was difficult for him. Firstly, being almost 20, he was older than most boys were when they started their apprenticeship. Secondly, he was already skilled in many aspects of the trade, and so did not really want to sign up for seven years, which was the length of time an apprentice was required to serve in those days. Thirdly, he wanted to be a financial burden on his father for as short a time as possible, given that business at home was not very healthy. Watt's aim was to complete his qualifications as quickly as possible and return to Glasgow to set up business himself and start earning some money.

A small break

After several weeks of searching, Watt finally found a man who would take him on and train him. John Morgan was willing to put aside the regulations of the Clock-makers, but for a price – Watt was to pay 20 **guineas** (£21) for a year's training in the art of mathematical instrument-making – and he had to work long hours. However, he achieved all he set out to do and qualified in the profession. There was a cost apart from money – the ten-hour days and lack of fresh air and exercise had left him in very poor health when, finally, in the summer of 1756, he headed back north to Scotland.

Glasgow University

Once his health had recovered, Watt made plans to set himself up in business in the city of Glasgow. Here he had another setback. He was thwarted by the **Corporation of Hammermen**, who said that he had not been born in the city nor qualified there. Help came once more from Glasgow University. The Hammermen did not have any power over who was employed there, and Professor Dick handed the young Watt a challenging task – to make and repair mathematical instruments for the university. He had already been paid the sum of £5 (a small fortune then) to repair and clean some astronomical instruments that had arrived at the university after a sea-trip from Jamaica. In the process, he made many new and influential friends who were to prove valuable to him later on. These friends included the chemist Dr Joseph Black and a student called John Robison.

Glasgow in the 18th century was a prosperous and growing city. Watt tried to set up in business here in 1756.

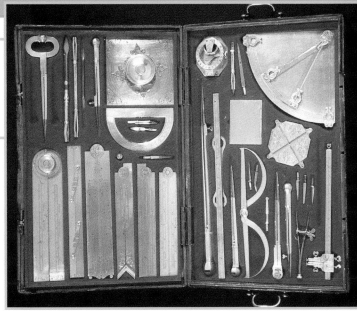

Watt made and mended mathematical and scientific instruments like these.

Holding his own

Not all Watt's time was spent in instrument repair or manufacture. He was an intelligent and educated young man, and those who came into contact with him recognized this. He was not simply a craftsman, but a potential scientist and inventor. He could hold his own in conversation with the best of the university men. It seems that they quickly came to accept him for the person he was. Perhaps for the first time since his education at the hands of his parents, he could be totally himself and feel at home and useful in his environment.

Money needs

The only major problem in Watt's life at this time seems to have been his ever-present need to earn more money. He made the decision to expand his business to include making and repairing musical, as well as mathematical, instruments. The plan worked. He even found the time to improve on some of the instruments that came to him – which showed that the skills of invention James had developed as a child were still there, and was a sign of the great things yet to come.

In his friends' words

Watt's friend Joseph Black wrote of him:

'He was as remarkable for the goodness of his heart, and the candour and simplicity of his mind, as for the acuteness of his genius and understanding.'

Perhaps more telling is the comment from John Robison, on his first impressions of Watt:

'I had the vanity to think myself a pretty good proficient in my favourite study [mathematics and mechanics], and was rather mortified at finding Mr Watt so much my superior. But his own high relish for those things made him pleased with the chat of any person who had the same tastes as himself.'

13

Marriage, and the steam engine

After a couple of years, Watt finally had his wish and opened an instrument-making shop in the city of Glasgow itself. He seems to have been accepted by the **Corporation of Hammermen**. At least, they did not object. He was even in a position to take on **apprentices** of his own. He still kept his workplace at Glasgow University, however. This was just as well, as the big break in his career came from that direction.

The revolutionary, though not very efficient, Newcomen steam engine at work. A model of this machine at Glasgow University started Watt on his famous career.

The Newcomen model engine

The university owned a model of a steam engine developed by a Devonshire blacksmith called Thomas Newcomen. It had been produced to pump water out of mines, a task that it performed moderately successfully. It was therefore a popular machine and it was bought by numerous mine-owners around the country. The university used the model as a demonstration piece in scientific classes. Late in 1763, Professor John Anderson came to Watt to see if he could help with repairing the model engine. He explained to the young man that the project had already defeated a London technician. The job would not be an easy one.

Taking up the challenge

Watt responded positively to this challenge. He seems to have relished the task. He was aware of the advances that had been made in terms of harnessing the power of steam. He was, after all, an instrument-maker, and deeply interested in practical science and mathematics. This was his world.

Here was an opportunity to grapple with one of the most revolutionary machines of his age. He was fascinated to see it at work. As he looked further into it, he started to conceive an ambitious plan – that of improving upon Newcomen's design. He managed to succeed in getting the model working satisfactorily again, but his mind moved beyond this and into the realms of genuine problem-solving.

The problem with Newcomen's pump, as Watt saw it, was to do with efficiency, or rather the lack of it. He saw quite clearly that the machine wasted a considerable amount of heat (energy) in the way it functioned, and efficient use of energy was the aim. Newcomen's machine was important in that it showed the potential power of steam. However, the machine was an early experiment in turning that potential into a practical reality. Watt saw that it could be designed differently to make it far more efficient. He quickly set himself the task of coming up with a practical solution to the problem.

Marriage

In 1764, James Watt married his cousin, Margaret Miller, a lively and cheerful woman, by all accounts. He was 28 years old and beginning to make his mark on the world. However, he was far from financially secure, and it was to be many years before he could earn money from the improvements he was making to the steam engine.

Early forms of power

As we have already seen, human civilizations all over the world had developed using three main sources of power – muscle, wind and water. This situation remained the same for thousands of years. Watt's Britain of the 18th century was very similar in this respect to the Britain of Shakespeare and Chaucer three or four centuries earlier. People had learned how to use these sources of power more efficiently. But the advancements had been patchy and slow in moving from one community to another.

Muscle power and civilization

From their most primitive stage, hundreds of thousands of years ago, people have used muscles to carry out necessary day-to-day tasks. The survival of individuals depends upon their ability to move – to find food and water, shelter, a mate, and to run away from danger, or to stand and fight off an attack – and the survival of the group depends on individuals' ability to use their muscles.

Humankind developed by finding more efficient ways of using this muscle power to carry out essential tasks. This, combined with increased understanding of the materials around us (such as wood, stone, bone, animal skins, and metals) and how they can be used, led to the growth of civilizations. Muscle power and natural resources were organized in such a way that some members of the community had the opportunity to develop other aspects of what we think of as 'civilization' – the arts (painting, drama, poetry, music), further labour-saving inventions, religion and philosophy, military tactics and expansion through the conquest of other territories. This is what we think of when we remember the civilizations of the Ancient Chinese, Greeks and Romans.

This engraving gives an idea of how the pyramids in Ancient Egypt were built over 4500 years ago using human muscle power.

Muscle power achieved its most impressive results through slavery. Thousands upon thousands of slaves were used to build the monuments of ancient civilizations. The pyramids of Ancient Egypt, the Great Wall of China and the Aztec temples are examples of these monuments that can still be seen today.

Wind and water

Ancient civilizations quickly learned how to harness the power of water. Using a water wheel to turn a grindstone, they could transform large quantities of grain into flour far more quickly than by using muscle power. A later invention was the windmill. This first came into use in Asia in the 7th century. Its use slowly spread into Europe, where windmills became a common sight by the 12th century. They were still very much in use in Watt's day.

Painting by Charles Calvert (1785–1852). Windmills were a common sight in Britain in the 18th century. They can still be found dotted across the countryside.

Limitations

Muscles, wind and water represented the limits of development. People could invent better ways of using them, but they could not overcome basic problems. Muscles (even those of strong animals, such as horses) tire out. Wind and water are unreliable (they can fail), and the mills had to be built where these sources of power were available.

A short history of steam

Steam power was revolutionary. Watt sensed its potential very quickly. It was to help change the foundations of modern civilizations and set them on a course of rapid industrialization.

Britain first

This process of industrialization happened first in Britain, where most of the early pioneering work on steam power was done. Steam provided people with a source of power that did not tire out, that could be transported to wherever it was needed, and that was relatively reliable. Steam was adaptable to the various uses industry wanted to make of it – in mines, in factories and on farms. Its output of energy was hundreds and even thousands of times the energy output of muscle power. However, neither Newcomen nor Watt were the first to experiment with it.

HERO'S AEOLIPILE

The first use of steam that we know of took place in Ancient Egypt. A Greek, named Hero of Alexandria, built a steam-powered machine called an aeolipile. It turned a sphere with two jets out of which the steam rushed. However, this successful experiment, carried out in about AD 100, was never applied to anything practical. It remained an interesting toy. Who knows how history may have turned out if Hero had used this machine to solve some of the engineering or agricultural problems of his day!

Almost 1500 years after Hero of Alexandria, in **Renaissance** Europe, experiments with steam still went no further than the production of small machines to amuse people. Giambattista della Porta (1535–1615) in Italy and Salomon de Caus (1576–1626) in England both built ingenious steam-powered toys.

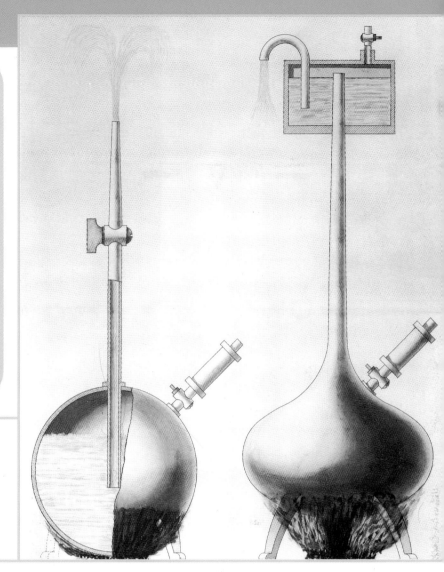

Steam-powered machines designed by Salomon de Caus in 1612. They had no practical purpose, but showed how steam could be put to work.

Steam and mining

A Frenchman named Denis Papin made a simple machine in 1690 that used steam to move it along the ground. Eight years later, an English military engineer called Thomas Savery took this principle and applied it to a practical problem of the day – that of pumping water out of mines in England. Thomas Newcomen built an even more successful steam-powered pump in 1712. This was the machine that Watt in turn improved upon in 1765. However, Newcomen's machine remained in use for most of the 18th century. It enabled mine-owners to dig deeper into the ground to find coal and metals such as tin, lead and iron. If flooding occurred, as it frequently did when the shaft was dug deep, the pump was used to remove the water. It could do this at a rate of about 2100 litres of water a minute.

Watt's separate condenser

When water is heated to boiling point, it turns into steam. Sir Samuel Morland, writing in 1690, said that 'The vapours from water evaporated by the force of fire demand incontinently a much larger space (about two thousand times) than the water occupied …'. This means that water expands when it becomes steam. This creates pressure and can be adapted to engineering purposes. Turning heat into mechanical energy is called **thermodynamics**. Watt needed to master this concept to improve the steam engine. When steam is changed back to water through cooling, it contracts. This can be used to create a **vacuum**. A **piston** in a metal cylinder can be moved simply by heating water and creating steam, pushing the piston up as it expands and allowing it to drop when the steam cools and contracts.

Atmospheric pressure

Another factor is atmospheric pressure. This pressure is all around us – it is literally the weight of the atmosphere bearing down on the earth and everything on it. It was proved to exist in 1654 by a German scientist, Otto von Guericke. He created a vacuum using steam, and showed that the force that moved the piston when steam was cooled came from the atmosphere itself.

A drawing of the experiment carried out by Otto von Guericke in 1654. Guericke placed two copper bowls together, forming a hollow sphere. When he removed the air from the sphere, teams of horses could not pull the bowls apart. This proved that there was tremendous air pressure pushing the bowls together.

Watt's ideas

Watt saw that Newcomen's pump used far too much heat to achieve results. It used the same metal chamber both for heating water into steam and for cooling the steam back into water. This was wasteful of precious energy, because the machine had to be constantly heated and cooled.

A diagram of James Watt's first steam engine, which had a separate condenser.

Newcomen's machine is called an **atmospheric engine**, because it uses the pressure of the atmosphere to force the piston back down. Condensing the steam was essential to creating a vacuum to allow this process to happen, but why not do it in a separate chamber? This was the key thought that came to Watt as he strolled around Glasgow Green, one fateful Sunday in May 1765. Using this method, the cylinder with the piston could be kept hot all the time – only the separate cooling chamber needed to be cold, so that the steam could condense back into water.

Proving his theory

Watt's task now was to prove this could be done, so he built a model in his workshop. It was a success! His machine was a true steam engine, in that both the up-stroke and the down-stroke of the piston were powered by steam. He did not rely upon atmospheric pressure to push the piston back down. This made the new steam engine three times as efficient as Newcomen's. In other words, it used a third of the amount of coal. This was of huge significance at the time. Steam engines were used in mines to pump out flood water. If it was a coal mine, the fuel for the machine was there on the doorstep. However, if it was a tin mine in Cornwall, coal had to be imported from other parts of the country to run the pumps. This was expensive. Watt's new engine would cut those costs by at least 60 per cent.

Family and money matters

James Watt was not able to make a full-scale finished steam engine of his own design, complete with separate condenser, until 1774. This was about nine years after he had successfully built a working model. The reasons for the delay were many. Watt had married in 1764 and had family responsibilities. This principally meant he had to earn enough money for his family's needs. He never found this aspect of life very easy. 'Nothing is more contrary to my disposition than bustling and bargaining ...,' he was to say of himself. He was an inventor, a dreamer with a practical genius, but he had no head for business. However, he had to apply himself to money matters, and the development of his steam engine was not showing any signs of generating income for the time being.

Watt's family

James and his wife Margaret were to have five children in all. John (born 1765) and Agnes (born 1770) both died as babies. Margaret (born 1767) and James (born 1769) both survived into adulthood. James, the son, lived until 1848, and inherited his father's business eventually. Watt's wife was to die in 1773, giving birth to their fifth child, who did not live.

Help from his friends

There was another practical problem that held back development of the steam engine, and that was the lack of skilled engineers and workmen to build a full-scale engine. Without finance and labour, Watt's chances of developing the engine looked very bleak indeed.

Dr John Roebuck (1718–94). Watt and Roebuck formed a partnership but it never quite worked out the way the two men had hoped.

However, once again, Watt's close friends were to lend a hand in shaping events. His friend Dr Joseph Black lent him money at this time and gave him tremendous encouragement. He saw that Watt was no ordinary engineer and instrument-maker. He saw also that his steam engine had huge potential, and therefore deserved to be made widely available to industry. He introduced Watt to John Roebuck, a scientist and industrialist, and the two men formed a business partnership.

Running out of steam

All seemed set to make progress. But it was not to be. The engineers at Roebuck's iron works were not up to the job of building a sophisticated steam engine, and Watt did not prove any good at organizing a team of men to work under his direction. Although an engine was put together at Roebuck's house, it did not function properly. Watt was forced to look elsewhere to earn money. From 1771, he became a **surveyor**, travelling all over Scotland, helping to build canals.

An 18th century painting of a canal. Canals were built all over Britain in the second half of the 18th century, changing the way people moved themselves and their goods around the country. Watt was for a while involved in helping build canals in his native Scotland.

DR JOHN ROEBUCK

Dr Black introduced Watt to Dr Roebuck in 1765. Roebuck was a scientist and industrialist. He had a **lease** on a coal mine at Kinneil, near Edinburgh, and ran the iron works at Carron, also in Scotland. He knew at first hand the problems with a mine that floods. He was therefore interested in a steam engine that worked quickly and efficiently pumping out mine shafts. Roebuck proposed a partnership – he would cover the costs of development and pay off any debts Watt had already incurred. In return, he would take two-thirds of all profits made from the venture.

Disappointment and tragedy

In August 1768, James Watt was introduced by Roebuck to Matthew Boulton, the most important industrialist in Britain at that time. This was to prove a fateful meeting. Watt's personality was the complete opposite of Boulton's. Watt was shy, doubtful and touchy. Boulton was confident, positive and successful. Boulton took to Watt, and saw very quickly the potential in his new steam engine. At this time, the deal with Roebuck was going nowhere. Boulton was willing to step in and take over the financial side of developing the pump. Unfortunately, nothing came out of the talks the three men had together.

*Matthew Boulton (1728–1809), factory owner and industrialist, aged about 73. His partnership with James Watt was one of the most important in the history of the early **Industrial Revolution**.*

The first patent

Roebuck, while not proving the financial force both Watt and Dr Black had hoped he would, nonetheless did have the sense to encourage Watt to apply for a **patent** for his engine. This he did, and the patent was granted in 1769. This meant that while the patent lasted, no one could copy the machine that Watt had invented. He was protected by law from anyone trying to pirate his invention. So, although the development of the steam engine seemed to be going nowhere, at least it was safe from the hands of others.

Bankruptcy

In 1772, John Roebuck went bankrupt. He had over-extended himself in his various industrial ventures. The failure of his business could have been the death-blow to Watt's dream of seeing his invention put to use. No work had been carried out on it for a long time – it was rotting away at Roebuck's Kinneil works. However, by chance one of the men that Roebuck owed money to was Matthew Boulton, who had already expressed interest in Watt's engine. Boulton agreed to write off the debt of £1200 in exchange for a partnership with Watt.

Personal tragedy

In September 1773, James was away when he heard that his wife, Margaret, was having a difficult childbirth. He made all haste to get back to her, but when he arrived, she and the new baby were both dead. He had been close to his wife and this tragedy struck him deeply. It was many months before he could turn his mind to other things, such as the future partnership with Boulton and the prospects for his engine. Margaret had been a great support to him through all the trials and disappointments over the development of his invention. He was to miss her in the years to come.

Margaret Watt, James's first wife. Her death in childbirth in 1773 was a great tragedy for James.

A productive partnership

Matthew Boulton (1728–1809) had set up the world's first factory at Soho, in Birmingham. He saw that to use his workers' time to the best advantage, they should all have a specific job to do in putting something together, and repeat that job over and over. In the past, workers had started and usually finished a complete job. Boulton gave workers only a part of the whole to work on. This was the birth of the factory system of mass production we all take for granted today. His factory turned out a variety of metal products, and he was soon to become 'the first manufacturer in England'.

Matthew Boulton was a rich man. He had inherited money and had also married a rich heiress. Nonetheless, he was not the sort of man to take life easy. He was interested in business and industry, and also in science. He had already corresponded with Watt on issues to do with steam engines, and was carrying out experiments of his own.

Watt moves south

It was into this environment of industry and successful results that Watt arrived in the spring following his wife's death. It must have lifted his heart to see the efficient Soho Manufactory, as it was called, and to feel the comfort of having enough money and resources put at his disposal to overcome all the problems he had encountered in the past. Boulton made workshops and skilled workmen available to Watt. They took the unsuccessful engine from Roebuck and started work on it once again.

Matthew Boulton's factory at Soho, Birmingham opened in 1765. This was one of the first, largest and most successful factories in the world.

This must have been a tremendous moment for the Scottish inventor. The depths of despair into which he had sunk only a few years previously must now have seemed firmly in the past. The future was looking far more positive, even to one with such a gloomy temperament as James Watt!

Working on the first engine

For two years, Watt applied himself to completing a working, full-scale, steam engine pump. His dream came true in 1776, when the first of many revolutionary engines came out of the Soho Manufactory. One of the first orders went to the then well-known ironmaster, John Wilkinson, who wanted to use it to operate the bellows at his iron works at Broseley. It was successful, and more orders for the steam engine came into the Soho Manufactory.

One of Watt's steam engines manufactured at the workshops of Boulton's Soho factory in Birmingham.

Interconnections

The world-changing movement known as the **Industrial Revolution** began in Britain in the mid-18th century. It was not an organized affair, but sprang up in various parts of the country over the years. Looking back on the men, the events and the inventions themselves, one thing becomes clear – although everything happened to some extent in a haphazard way, some events were interconnected. One invention and its consequences led on to another invention, and on to further consequences.

As steam engines and other machines became more complicated to build, special tools like this metal-planing machine were designed to help with the task.

Watt and Wilkinson

An example of this is the relationship between Watt and John Wilkinson. Watt's steam engine provided Wilkinson's iron works with far more controllable power than it had ever had previously. This allowed the iron works to expand and become even more successful. But Wilkinson's business also benefited Watt and his engine. Finding skilled workers to build the engine parts had been a problem for Watt from the very beginning. Boulton largely solved this problem by providing him with men who had the necessary skill. But Wilkinson solved one special problem for Watt – how to manufacture an accurate and safe cylinder. Wilkinson had developed an industrial technique for **boring** cannon. This had grown out of the needs of the British army and navy for accurate cannons (used later in the **Napoleonic Wars**). The same technique was applied to the manufacture of Watt's cylinders, with great success.

Machine tools

One of the single most important areas of development during the 19th century was that of **machine tools**. As more machines were being built, more tools were needed to help build them. As machines became increasingly sophisticated, so machine tool manufacture had to keep pace. There were half a dozen well-known scientists who were active in this field at the time of Watt. They all knew each other, and most had worked for or with each other. They were Joseph Bramah, Henry Maudsley, Joseph Clement, Joseph Whitworth, James Nasmyth and Marc Isambard Brunel. Between them, these men set the standards for manufacturing machine tools and training a workforce in Britain capable of producing the tools to make the most complicated machines of the day – including the steam engine.

Inventions during Watt's day could only be manufactured if the right materials, tools, and people to use them were available. Many inventions in the past had come to nothing, because, although the ideas were based on sound science and mechanics, the means were not there to do anything with them. Some of the most famous examples are the inventions of Leonardo da Vinci (1452–1519), which included a flying machine and a submarine. They remained ideas on paper and dreams in the genius inventor's head, but were never built.

Closer to Watt's time was Charles Babbage (1792–1871). He is called the 'father of the computer', and although he went a long way with the mathematical theory, he found it impossible to construct a complete machine, given the lack of suitable materials and the low level of development of precision machine tools at the time.

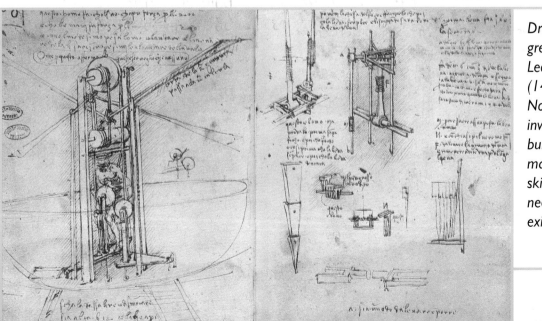

Drawings by the great genius Leonardo da Vinci (1452–1519). None of his inventions were built because the materials and skilled workers needed did not exist at the time.

Steam power takes off

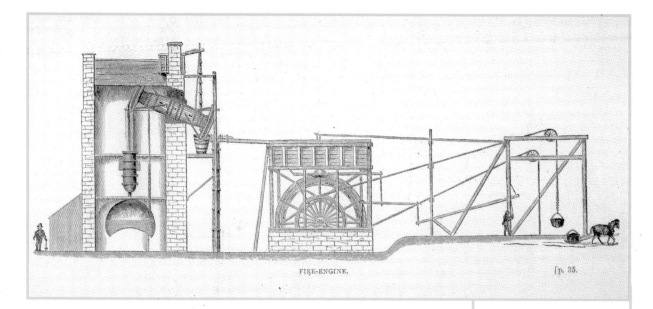

FIRE-ENGINE.   [p. 35.

As a result of the Boulton and Watt partnership, around 500 steam engines were produced by 1800. This amounted to about half the total number of steam engines in use at the time. The Age of Steam was well and truly under way by now. It was really set in action in 1776 when Watt's engine showed the world just how powerful steam could be. Over the coming years, Watt was to work on his original design, adding significant improvements. However, for the moment, Boulton could be justifiably proud of his foresight and shrewd business judgement, and Watt could be delighted with his success at last.

A Boulton and Watt steam pump at work. Its success was due to its efficient use of coal and its capacity to remove great quantities of water from deep mines.

Publicity and success

The engine built for Wilkinson was quickly followed by others. The owners of the Bentley Mining Company put in an order for one and quickly had it up and running in 1776. Its first operation attracted a lot of attention. A great crowd gathered to watch. In that crowd was a newspaper reporter who was to write up what he saw. All went well, and news about Watt's engine spread fast throughout the mining community. Now orders started to come in thick and fast.

Remarriage and Cornwall

James Watt remarried in 1776. Ann MacGregor was the sister-in-law of a Glasgow friend, Gilbert Hamilton, who probably introduced them in the first place. James and Ann lived together at Harper's Hill, James's home since his move to Birmingham two years earlier.

Ann was quickly introduced to her new world – the couple undertook an arduous four-day journey to Cornwall to oversee the installation of Watt's engines in the county. Cornish mine-owners had already attempted to steal the design of the engine and make it their own. They had sent men to look at the machine working at another mine. However, they were thwarted in their plan and had to settle for the legal approach. But they did not make Watt and his wife welcome, in spite of their 200-mile trip. And Watt was back doing what he least enjoyed – working amongst people, ordering affairs and conducting business.

Tin and copper were mined in Cornwall. The mines there were prone to flooding. When Watt arrived in the summer of 1777, they had 75 Newcomen engines helping to pump water. Six years later, there was only one Newcomen engine still in use. The far more efficient Watt engine had replaced all the others. The Cornish miners had to import expensive coal to fuel their steam pump engines. Anything that saved them using so much of this precious fuel was a big help to their industry.

A drawing of a Cornish tin mine in the 18th century. Coal, used to power the steam pumps, was expensive in Cornwall because it had to be brought from far away.

Rotary motion and other improvements

Watt made the first improvement to his engine in 1781. He worked out a process whereby he could use steam to power the **piston** in the cylinder on both the up-stroke and the down-stroke. Before, his engine had supplied power only to the down-stroke, using gravity to supply the up-stroke. His new double-acting piston gave almost twice as much power to his engine, for the same amount of fuel used – an incredible advantage over other machines.

The need for rotary motion

Watt's original design was for what is called a *reciprocating engine* – one which has both up and down movement. This is all that was required of it in the mines, where pumping water was the task being performed. However, Boulton (ever the businessman!) saw early on that the engine had the potential to be adapted to meet the needs of many different industries that were springing up around the country. But design alterations would be necessary, especially one that turned the up-and-down motion into rotary motion (that is, a movement that goes round and round).

Boulton had his eye on the booming cotton and wool textile industries. Cornwall had been a lucrative market, but it was now saturated with their engines. Boulton was determined to find other uses for them. New inventions had mechanized the process of producing cotton and woollen fabrics. But the new mills were still using water to power their looms and spinning frames. Boulton saw that there was an opportunity here.

A drawing of a cotton mill using steam instead of water to power the looms.

This machine shows the gears that produced rotary motion, which was essential for use in cotton and wool mills.

In Boulton's words

Boulton saw that to keep on selling their invention, they 'would have to find new markets'. He wrote to Watt saying:

'There is no other Cornwall to be found, and the most likely line for the consumption of our engines is the application of them to mills which is certainly an extensive field.'

Steam power could replace water power, but the steam engine would need to be able to supply rotary (circular) motion to make it successful in the mills. He wrote to Watt in June 1781, saying:

'The people in London, Manchester and Birmingham are steam mill mad. I don't mean to hurry you but I think in the course of a month or two, we should determine to take out a **patent** for certain methods of producing rotative motion ...'

Cracking the problem

Watt set about the problem of turning up-and-down motion into circular motion. He finally achieved this by working out what was later called *parallel motion*. By using a system of gears, he could use the movement of a straight beam to operate a wheel that went round. He told his son James in later life, 'I am not over anxious after fame. Yet I am more proud of the parallel motion than of any other mechanical invention I have ever made.'

Measuring energy

James Watt in the 1790s, now a rich man celebrated by his countrymen for his steam engine designs, and hailed as an engineering genius.

One aspect of producing steam engines on an industrial scale for a variety of customers was that of comparing their power and efficiency. Watt thought about this problem. Up to this point in time, there had been no need to worry about any standard measure as such. Wind, water, human and animal muscles, the odd machine – these were the power sources for farming and industry. The scale of operation at any one place was generally small. Power was important, but more in terms of overcoming its unreliability than measuring it. With the advent of powerful, steam-driven engines that could work night and day, output of products increased considerably. Different types of machine were to come on to the market. The need to know just how powerful any one machine was became an issue. But what standard unit of output or energy could be used and how could it be defined?

Horse power

The standard notion of output of energy in use at this time was that of the work a horse could do. When a sawmill owner came to Watt to order an engine, he explained what he wanted in terms of how much work his horses were doing in the mill. After all, the engine was going to replace them. He wanted something that would cope with the work of twelve horses. Watt, with his rigorous mind, set about putting this rather vague notion onto a proper scientific footing. He first needed to find out how much work an average horse could actually do. His calculations led him to the conclusion that the power of a horse could be measured as being able to lift 33,000 pounds (14,850 kilograms) the distance of one foot (30.5 centimetres) in one minute. Horsepower (shortened to hp) was to become the standard British imperial measurement of power, used to describe how powerful any machine was.

Watt based his unit of power on the amount of work one horse needed to do to lift 33,000 pounds (14,850 kg) 1 foot (30.5 cm).

THE WATT

As science and industry moved on, so a new unit of power was needed to define output or consumption or energy on a much smaller scale. The scientific community named it the watt, in honour of James Watt himself. One unit of horsepower, the original measurement of power, is equivalent to 746 watts.

Impact on industry and society

James Nasmyth's mighty steam hammer at work in an iron foundry in the first half of the 19th century.

In Watt's words

This is how James Watt saw the effect of his improved, more flexible machine – the double-acting rotative engine – on the industries of Britain:

'In most of our great manufactories these engines now supply the place of water, wind, and horse mills; and, instead of carrying the work to the power, the prime agent is placed wherever it is most convenient to the manufacturer.'

By the early 19th century, steam power was having an influence on all the major industries of the country – mining, textiles, milling, iron and steel production, and printing. It was paving the way for Britain to become 'the workshop of the world'. For example, between 1788 and 1804 steam power enabled the iron industry in Britain to increase its output by 400 per cent. Iron was used, amongst other things, to build machines. Many machines were now steam-driven, so more of them could be built. In this way one development fed another.

Rapid development

James Watt's inventions contributed enormously to the industrial developments going on around him. These developments were to affect the lives of every man, woman and child in Britain.

The growth of the engineering industries that produced and maintained steam engines helped other industries develop more quickly than they otherwise would have done. Increased iron and coal production in turn helped the engineering industry. Mass-produced textiles and other goods became more widely available at lower prices than ever before. Transport gradually developed, firstly through canal building in the late 18th century, and eventually through better road construction and the rapid growth of the steam railways from the 1830s onwards. Agriculture was also changed by the introduction of steam-driven machines – for **threshing** wheat, for example. And better transport widened the **markets** for agricultural produce.

Watt remained to the end of his life immensely proud of his contribution to all this progress.

The cotton industry became the first to use steam power for all the main stages of production. This is significant, because by 1810 this industry was the biggest in Britain, and therefore the world. By 1830, it made up about half of all the exports Britain made. It was cheaper to ship raw cotton from India to Britain, where it was made into cloth, and export it back to the Indian market, than it was for people in India to use their own raw cotton and turn it into cloth for themselves!

This drawing of the trial of a new steam plough shows how steam came to revolutionize farm machinery as well as that of industry.

A rival engineer – Richard Trevithick

Richard Trevithick (1771–1833), who was a great Cornish mining engineer and rival of Watt's for a time.

James Watt's biggest rival during his lifetime was probably the mining engineer Richard Trevithick (1771–1833). Trevithick was born in Cornwall, in the heart of tin and copper mining country, amongst people whose livelihoods came from the mines.

Trevithick saw the great effect that Watt's steam pump had on conditions underground. It extracted more dangerous flood water at a cheaper cost than before, enabling the mines to be dug deeper and deeper. However, mine-owners still had to buy the machinery and pay a **royalty** on fuel savings. Boulton had taken out a **patent** that lasted until 1800, which was 31 years after the first engine was installed. As time went on, the Cornish mine-owners began to resent paying this royalty. One legal way round it was to design an engine of their own, which did not infringe upon Watt's **copyright** in any way.

WORKING OUT THE SUMS

The Boulton and Watt company produced their steam engines to order. They designed each machine according to the needs of the customer. They then installed the engine and made sure that it was working properly. For all this work, they made a charge. But they also charged a royalty for the patent they had on the machine. This was calculated as one-third of the saving in fuel made by their engine compared with a Newcomen engine of the same power. However, mine-owners, especially the Cornish, often resented paying this royalty and Watt for a while had the distasteful job of chasing payments. Eventually, this task was handed over to William Murdock, the **foreman**, who proved much better suited to it than Watt!

High-pressure engines

One of the largest contributions Trevithick made to the world of steam was the building of a high-pressure engine. Newcomen's engines were **atmospheric engines**. Watt improved on these, but still only used low pressure. Trevithick, having built the first full-scale **locomotive** in 1801, went on to build one that used pressure of 145 pounds (66 kilograms) per square inch (6½ square centimetres) – a tremendous feat for the time. But unfortunately for him, the event did not catch the attention of the world and he gave up experimenting.

Danger and death

Trevithick did continue to build fixed high-pressure engines for a variety of uses. However, disaster struck when one exploded at a corn mill in Greenwich, London, in 1803. This is how Trevithick wrote of the event, with the spellings that he used:

An early 19th century engraving of Richard Trevithick's 'Portable Steam Engine'.

'It appears the boy that had care of the engine was gon to catch eales … and left the care of it to one of the Labourers; this labourer saw the engine working much faster than usual, stop'd it without takeing off a spanner which fastned down the steam lever, and a short time after being Idle it burst. It killed three on the spot and one other is sence dead … I beleive that Mr B [Boulton] and Watt is abt to do mee every engurey [injury] in their power for they have don their outemost to repoart the exploseion both in the newspapers and private letters …'

There was no love lost between the rival engineers. Trevithick, in spite of his inventions, died a poor man in 1833. However, his more powerful, high-pressure engines paved the way for later developments in transport. Both railway and ship engineers were to use them.

Old age and contentment

James Watt retired from his profitable business partnership with Matthew Boulton at the age of 64 in 1800, the year his **patent** on the separate condenser steam engine expired. He went to live out the remaining years of his life at his home, Heathfield House, near Birmingham, which he had had built. In the attic was a workshop, where he still spent plenty of time. He also took to pastimes that he had not had as much time in the past to enjoy. These included planning and looking after a large garden, planting trees and tending a greenhouse. He had had two children by his second wife – Janet and Gregory. Janet had already died aged 15 in 1794. Gregory was a handsome boy and showed great intellectual promise. However, he too was to die young, in 1804, aged 27. This was a great blow to Watt in his retirement.

James Watt's home, Heathfield House, near Birmingham. He retired here to live out his old age in some contentment.

Still inventing

Before he retired, Watt had worked out a way to mass-copy written pages of work. 'I have fallen on a way of copying writing chemically,' he said. In retirement, he started work on a process for copying sculpture. He tried designing a machine that would do the work. His mind was still active and able to take in new ideas and see how far he could get with them. The difference was that there was no financial pressure upon him any more. He could indulge his creativity in a way that had not been possible in his younger days.

Passing on the business

Both Matthew Boulton (who died in 1809) and James Watt passed on their share of the business to their sons, Matthew Robinson Boulton and James Watt (junior). James Watt the younger had received a good education and sound workshop training before he entered fully into the business. James Watt the elder could rest assured that the business he had struggled so long to build up would remain in good hands. He had come a long way from his days as a young man struggling to break into the instrument-makers' **apprenticeship** system in London and Glasgow. He had also made sure that his son would not have to take the same route to achieve his dreams.

In a contemporary's words

In the event, Watt's twilight years were long, as he lived to the age of 83. He had had an unpromising start in life, with his illness and frailty. This was how a contemporary described James Watt as an adult:

'... *his shoulders stooping and his chest falling in, his limbs lank and unmuscular, and his complexion sallow .... His utterance was slow and low in tone, with a broad Scottish accent; his manners gentle, modest, and unassuming.*'

But in spite of this physical weakness, he had won success with his inventions, fame in the eyes of the world, and material comfort.

James Watt later in life, a successful and contented man.

Following Watt's death in August 1819, at the grand age of 83, **obituaries** were written by those who saw the influence of his inventions all around them. It is clear from the tone and content of these obituaries that Watt was held in high regard. And Watt's belief in his inventions and dogged determination to see them through, even at a cost to his health, were recognized by society during his lifetime as much as after it. Few inventors of the period had been so well rewarded, both financially and in terms of awards. He was a Fellow of both the Edinburgh and London **Royal Societies**. Glasgow University gave him an honorary degree in 1806, and in 1814 he was made one of the few foreign associates of the highly regarded French Academy.

Economic and political legacy

The sincere belief in the future benefits of mechanical and industrial progress expressed in Watt's obituaries was partly due to the gains already made from this progress. Watt had changed things for ever, and mechanical power was clearly seen as the path forward. There would be no turning back. Society at large was gaining economically from advances in industry and agriculture. Mass production brought prices down, which made goods available to more people. There was a significant growth in the middle classes during this period. As they became more powerful, so they gained greater confidence and demanded more say in the running of the country. Out of this came political reform, one of the main advances being the widening of the voting population to include the middle classes in 1832.

Steam power brought down the cost of mass-produced factory textiles like these bolts of tweed.

Transport

In the 18th century, transport of one form or another was not new – horses and carriages had been around for thousands of years. But steam transformed transport. Steam power paved the way for a whole host of new advances. Some took place in new arenas, but others transformed old ones. For example, experiments in building steam-powered machines that could move along a road dated back to 1770.

Wooden rails had been in use since the Middle Ages. But the combination of a steam engine and metal rails was to change the nature of rail transport totally. Richard Trevithick was doing experiments during Watt's lifetime. He built a **locomotive** in 1803. In the 1820s, pioneers such as George Stephenson took things much further. The Stockton and Darlington Railway opened in 1825, the first of many. By 1840, there were about 1500 kilometres (900 miles) of track in Britain. Ten years later, there was seven times as much track in existence.

Steam boats became popular in the 1820s, and the first steam-powered crossing of the Atlantic took place in 1838. In 1854, Isambard Kingdom Brunel (1806–59) built this ship, SS Great Britain, the first steam ship with an iron hull.

Changing the world

Through invention and innovation, James Watt helped shape the world that we have inherited. We no longer count steam as our main source of energy. Things have moved on and we have electricity and nuclear power, as well as fossil fuels such as oil and gas. But Watt realized more clearly than most that harnessing power was the key to technological, economic and material advancement.

Timeline

c. AD 100	Hero of Alexandria experiments with the power of steam.
1690	The Frenchman Denis Papin makes a simple machine powered by steam.
1698	The English military engineer Thomas Savery patents his steam-powered water-pump, called the 'Miner's Friend'.
1712	Thomas Newcomen builds the first 'atmospheric' steam pump, which is set to work at a mine near Dudley in Staffordshire, England.
1736	James Watt is born on 19 January at Greenock, near Glasgow, Scotland.
1754	Watt starts his training as a scientific instrument-maker in Glasgow.
1755	Moves to London to seek an apprenticeship in instrument-making. Spends a year learning his craft under John Morgan in Cornhill, London.
1756	Returns to Scotland to find work at Glasgow University repairing an instrument collection.
1757	Given the role of 'Mathematical Instrument Maker' to the University of Glasgow and opens a shop on the premises.
1763	Given a model of Newcomen's atmospheric steam pump to repair. He begins to understand its weaknesses.
1764	Marries Margaret Miller.
1765	In May, finally 'cracks' the problem of improving on Newcomen's design, adding a separate cooling chamber (or condenser). Introduced to John Roebuck, scientist and industrial businessman.
1767	Starts as a surveyor on canal-building projects.
1769	Enters into partnership with Roebuck, who encourages him to take out a patent on his separate condenser. Meets Matthew Boulton in Birmingham, England.
1773	John Roebuck becomes bankrupt. Margaret Miller, Watt's wife, dies in childbirth.
1774	Watt enters into partnership with Matthew Boulton and moves to Birmingham, England.
1776	Watt and Boulton build their first working steam pump for commercial use. Watt marries Ann MacGregor.

1777	Travels with his new wife to Cornwall to set up his steam pumps at mines in the county.
1780	Takes out a patent on his letter-copying process.
1781–2	Takes out a patent on other improvements he makes to the steam engine – the sun and planet gears for the rotative engine.
1782	Develops a standard unit for measuring output of power – the horsepower.
1783	Builds the first rotative engine.
1785	Elected a Fellow of the Royal Society.
1800	The patent on the Watt and Boulton steam engine runs out. Watt and Bouton's partnership comes to an end. Watt retires at the age of 64.
1809	Death of Matthew Boulton.
1819	James Watt dies on 25 August.

Places to visit and further reading

Places to visit
The Science Museum, London (includes three Watt steam engines and a reconstruction of his attic at Heathfield House)

Papplewick Pumping Station, Ravenshead, Notts (includes Watt pumping engines)

The Science Museum, Birmingham

The Royal Society, London

Kew Bridge Steam Museum, London (includes Boulton & Watt engine pump)

Further reading

McTavish, Douglas: *James Watt* – Pioneers of Science series (Wayland, Hove, 1992)

Sproul, Anna: *James Watt* – Scientists Who Have Changed the World series (Exley, 1992)

Tames, Richard: *The Steam Engine: A Breakthrough in Energy* – Turning Points in History series (Heinemann Library, Oxford, 1998)

Glossary

apprentice someone bound to an employer for a set number of years to learn a craft or a trade

atmospheric engine machine that uses the pressure of atmosphere to make it work

bore make a hole in something or enlarge an existing hole

copyright sole right, due to ownership, to produce something and make money out of it

Corporation of Hammermen Scottish guild of craftsmen involved with making tools and instruments

craft guilds organizations of craft workers and merchants, started in the Middle Ages, that aimed to set standards for various types of crafts and help their members

foreman person who organizes workers in industry

grammar school originally, a school in England in which Latin grammar and other languages were taught. The term is still used in England for secondary schools where more academically able pupils may go.

guinea gold coin in use in Britain from 1717 to 1813, worth 21 shillings (£1.05)

Industrial Revolution name given to a series of changes and inventions in industry in Britain that led to the growth of factories and increased output of manufactured goods. The Industrial Revolution began to make itself felt from about 1760 onwards.

infant mortality rate at which babies up to the age of one year die. This is usually expressed as so many deaths in 1000 births. The figure was very high in the 18th century, but dropped significantly in the 19th century.

lease contract allowing the use of land or a building for a specified time

locomotive early steam engine that moved along by its own power

logarithms numbers used in tables to help people work out complicated sums quickly. Logarithmic tables were popular before the invention of the calculator.

machine tool machine used to make parts made of metal

market opportunity for buying or selling

migraine acute headache that makes the sufferer feel sick and unable to bear any light

Napoleonic Wars series of wars that took place between about 1803 and 1815, in which the Emperor of France, Napoleon I, fought other European nations, including Britain, Austria, Russia, Prussia and Sweden

obituary record made of a person's life shortly after they have died, usually in a newspaper

patent the right of a person or company to make, sell and use an invention they have produced, for a certain period of time

piston barrel-shaped piece of metal that moves up and down in a cylinder in most engines

quadrant instrument used for measuring the altitude of stars

Renaissance period in European history that marked the end of the Middle Ages and the start of the modern world. It saw a growth in science, art and literature, and a rediscovery of the Classics (Ancient Greek and Roman writings and ideas). It started in Italy in the 14th century, and was at its height 200 years later.

Royal Society most prestigious scientific society in Britain

royalty payment made to a person for the right to use something they have invented or produced

shipwright person involved in building ships

surveyor person who inspects land with a view to building on it or developing it and who organizes a workforce to carry out work on it

thermodynamics the study of the relationship between heat and mechanical work

threshing separating grain from the rest of the plant by beating it

vacuum space or area that is empty of all matter, including gases

Worshipful Company of Clock-makers London guild of craftsmen involved with making tools and instruments, as well as clocks

Index

agriculture 4, 37
ancient civilizations 16–17
atmospheric engines 21, 39
atmospheric pressure 20

Babbage, Charles 29
Black, Dr Joseph 12, 13, 23
Boulton, Matthew 5, 7, 24, 25, 26, 27, 28, 30, 32, 33, 38, 41
Bramah, Joseph 29
Brunel, Isambard Kingdom 43
Brunel, Marc Isambard 29

canals 23, 37
Clement, Joseph 29
coal mining 21, 37
copyright 24, 38
Corporation of Hammermen 12, 14
cotton industry 33, 37
cylinders 20, 28, 32

de Caus, Salomon 18, 19
della Porta, Giambattista 19
Dick, Professor Robert 10, 12

energy output 34, 35
energy sources 4, 5, 16–17
England in the 18th century 4, 16

factory system 26
French Academy 42

gears 32, 33
Glasgow University 10, 12, 14, 42

Hero of Alexandria 19
high-pressure engines 39
horsepower (hp) 35

Industrial Revolution 4, 5, 28
industrialization 18
infant mortality 6
instrument-making 9, 10, 11
iron industry 27, 28, 36, 37

Leonardo da Vinci 29
locomotives 39, 43

machine tools 28, 29
mass production 26, 37, 42
Maudsley, Henry 29
middle classes 42
mining industry 5, 14, 19, 21, 23, 30, 31, 32, 38
Morland, Sir Samuel 20
muscle power 4, 16–17

Napier, John 7
Napoleonic Wars 28
Nasmyth, James 29, 36
Newcomen, Thomas 14, 18
Newcomen engine 14–15, 19, 21, 31, 38, 39
Newton, Isaac 6, 7

Papin, Denis 19
parallel motion 33
patents 24, 33, 38, 39, 40
piston 20, 21, 32
political reform 42

railways 37, 39, 43
reciprocating engine 32
Robison, John 12, 13
Roebuck, Dr John 22, 23, 24, 25
rotary motion 32, 33
rotative engine 36
Royal Society 42
royalties 38

Savery, Thomas 19
slavery 16, 17
Soho Manufactory 26, 27
steam boats 43
steam engine 21, 22, 23, 24, 26, 27, 28, 30, 32, 34, 37, 38
steam power 5, 14, 15, 18–19, 30, 36, 42, 43
steam pump 14, 21, 23, 27, 38, 30
steam-powered toys 18, 19
Stephenson, George 43

textile industry 5, 32, 33, 37, 42
thermodynamics 20
tin mining 21, 31
transport 23, 37, 43
Trevithick, Richard 38, 39, 43

von Guericke, Otto 20

water power 4, 5, 17, 33
water wheels 5, 17
Watt, Ann 31
Watt, James
  achievements and legacy 5, 37, 42
  birth and early life 4, 6–7, 8–9
  canal surveyor 23
  death 42
  develops the steam engine 21, 22, 23, 24, 26, 27, 28, 30, 32
  education 6–7, 8–9
  ill health 6
  instrument-making business 9, 10–11, 12, 13, 14
  marriages and children 15, 22, 25, 31, 40
  partnership with Matthew Boulton 5, 7, 24, 25, 26, 27, 30, 32, 33, 40
  personal qualities 7, 13, 24
  pessimism 8, 27
  public recognition 42
Watt, James (junior) 22, 41
Watt, Margaret 15, 22, 25
watts 35
Whitworth, Joseph 29
Wilkinson, John 27, 28
wind power 4, 17
windmills 4, 17
Worshipful Company of Clock-makers 11